This Coloring Book Belongs To

____

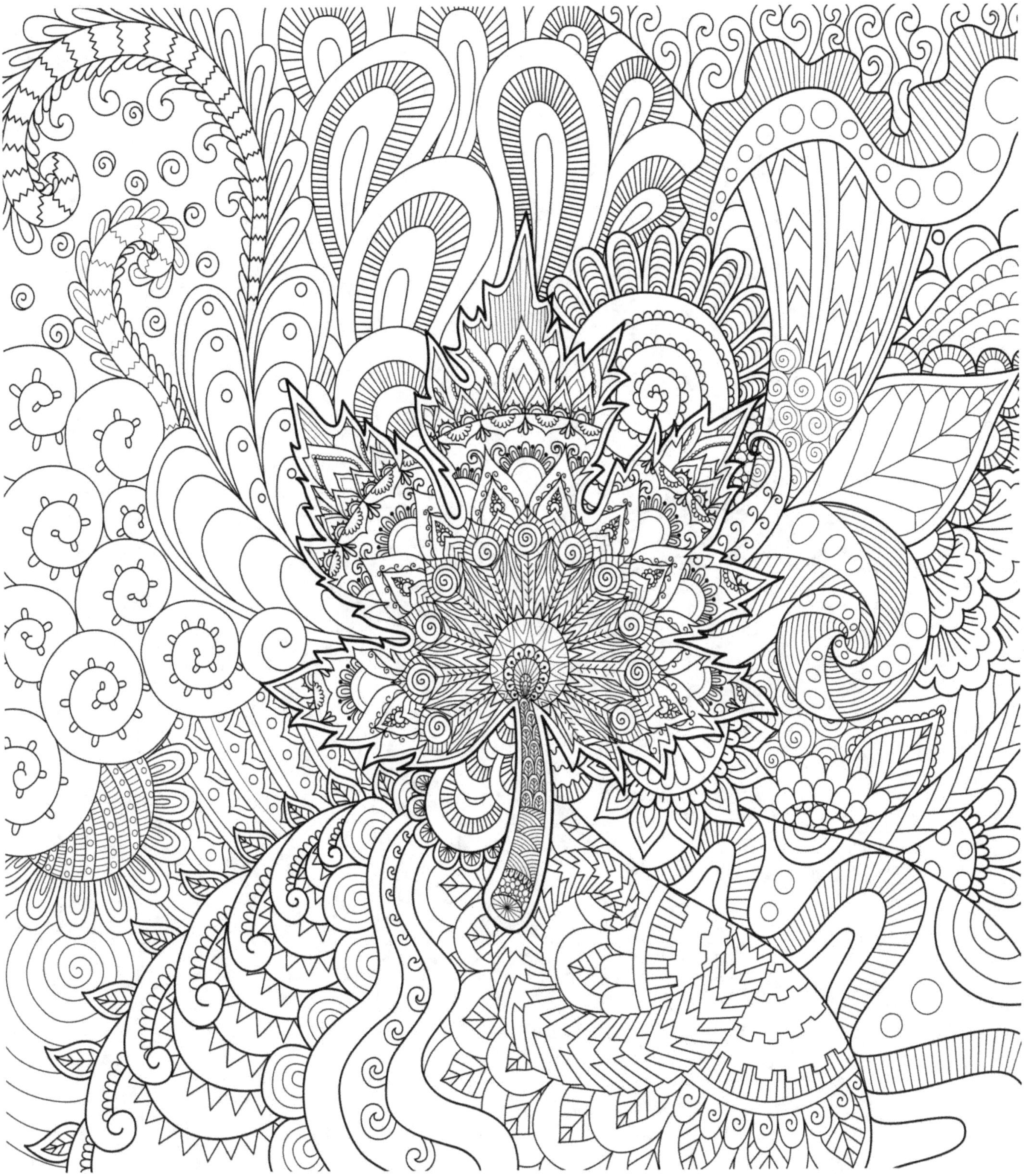

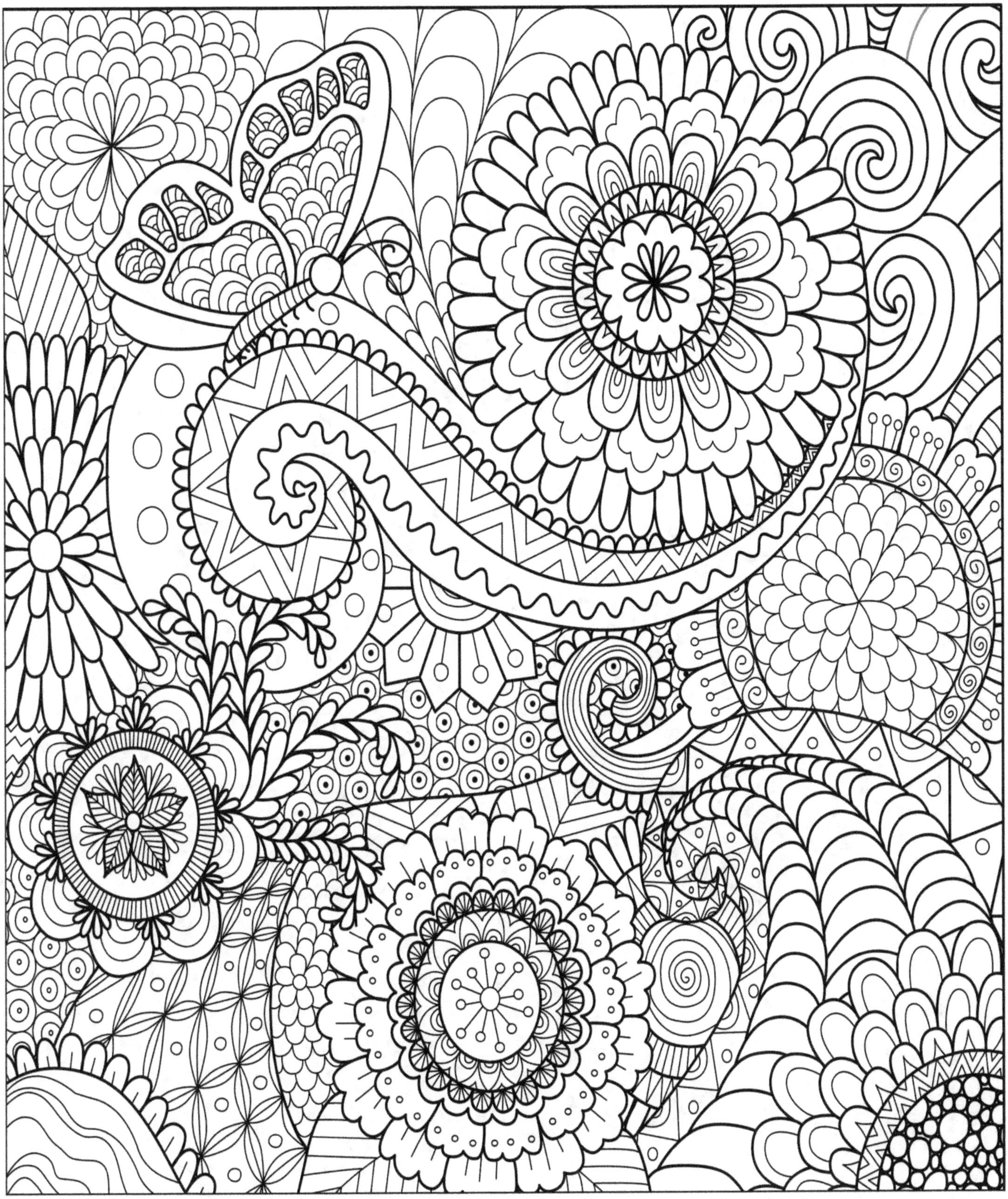

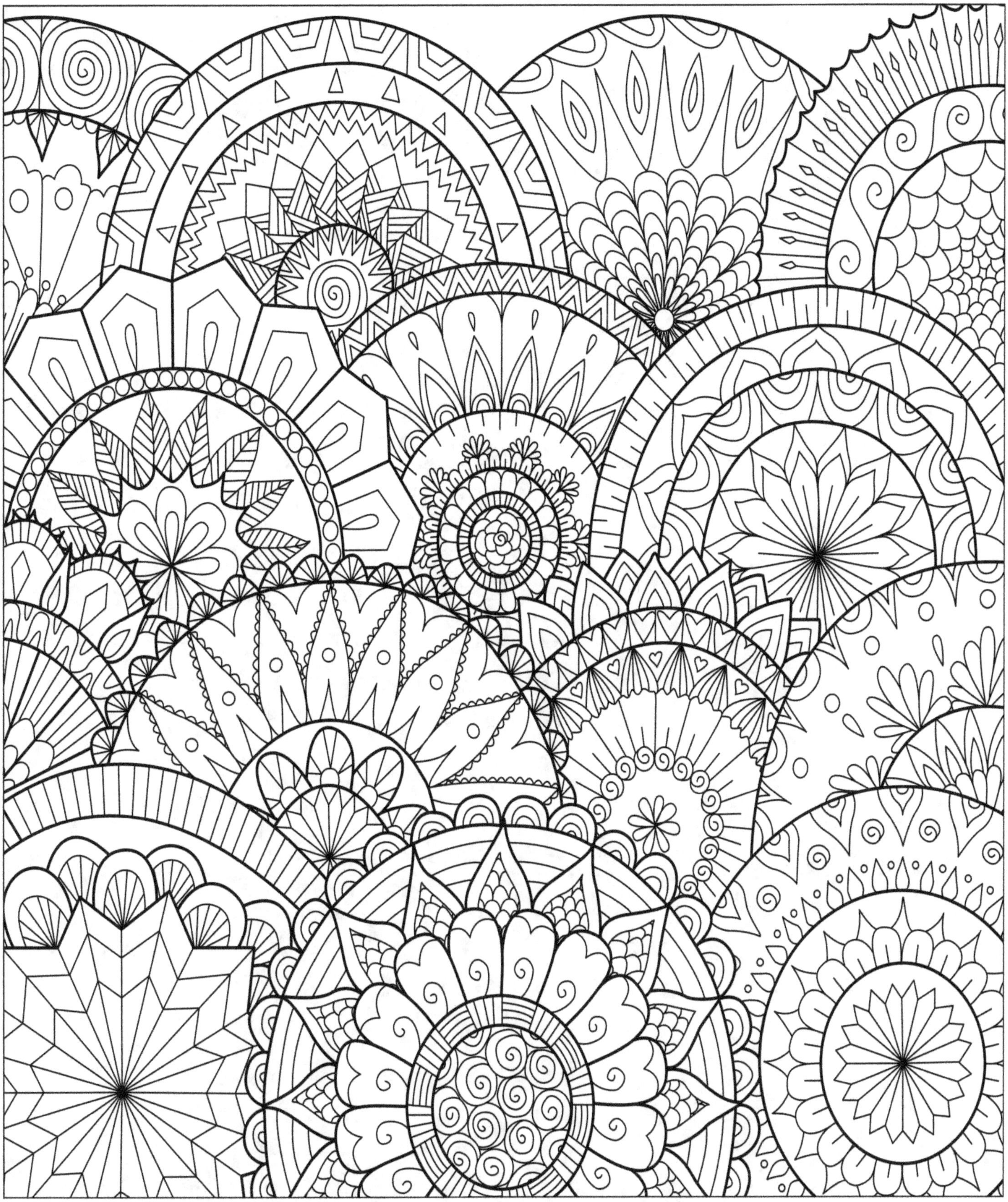

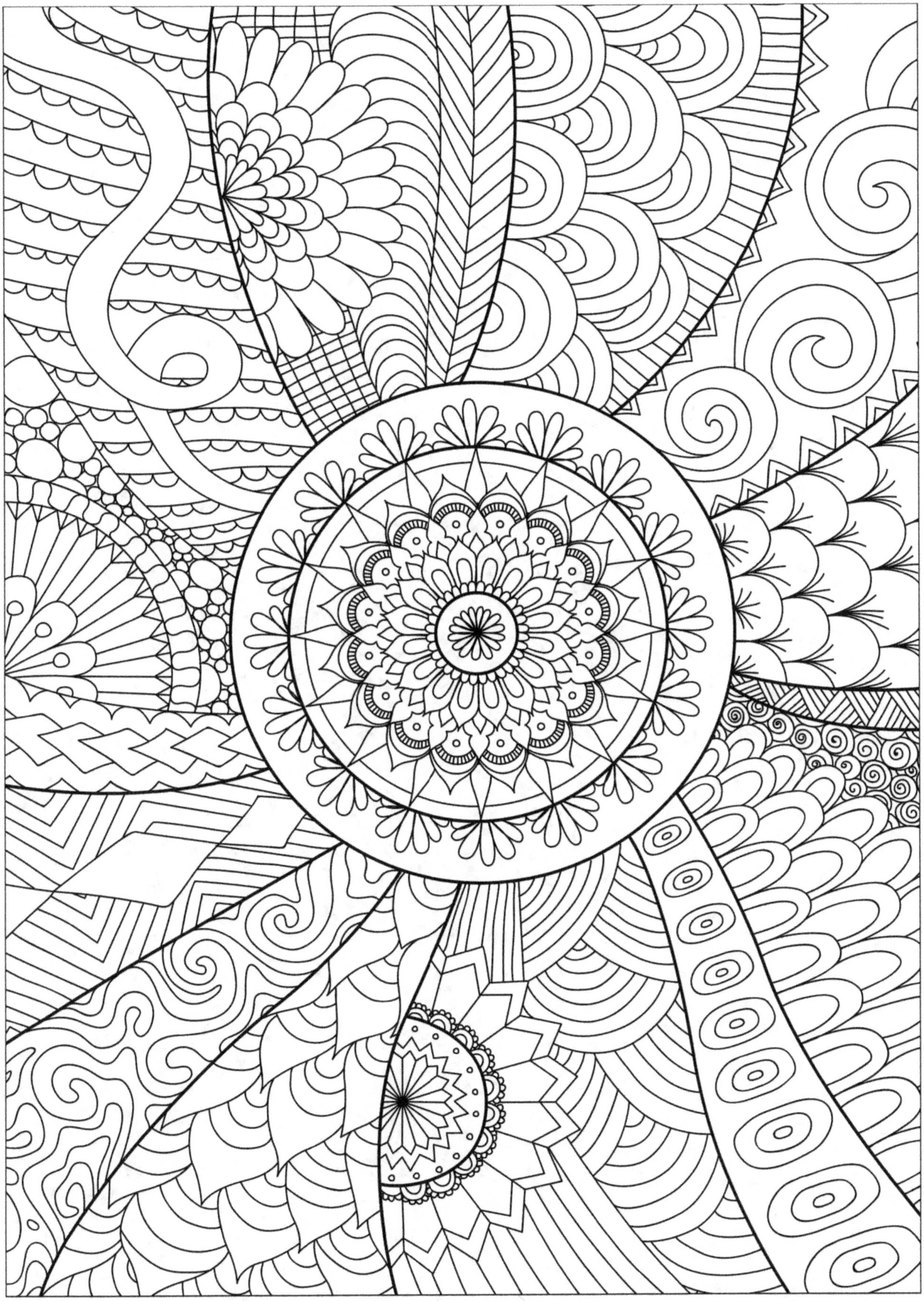

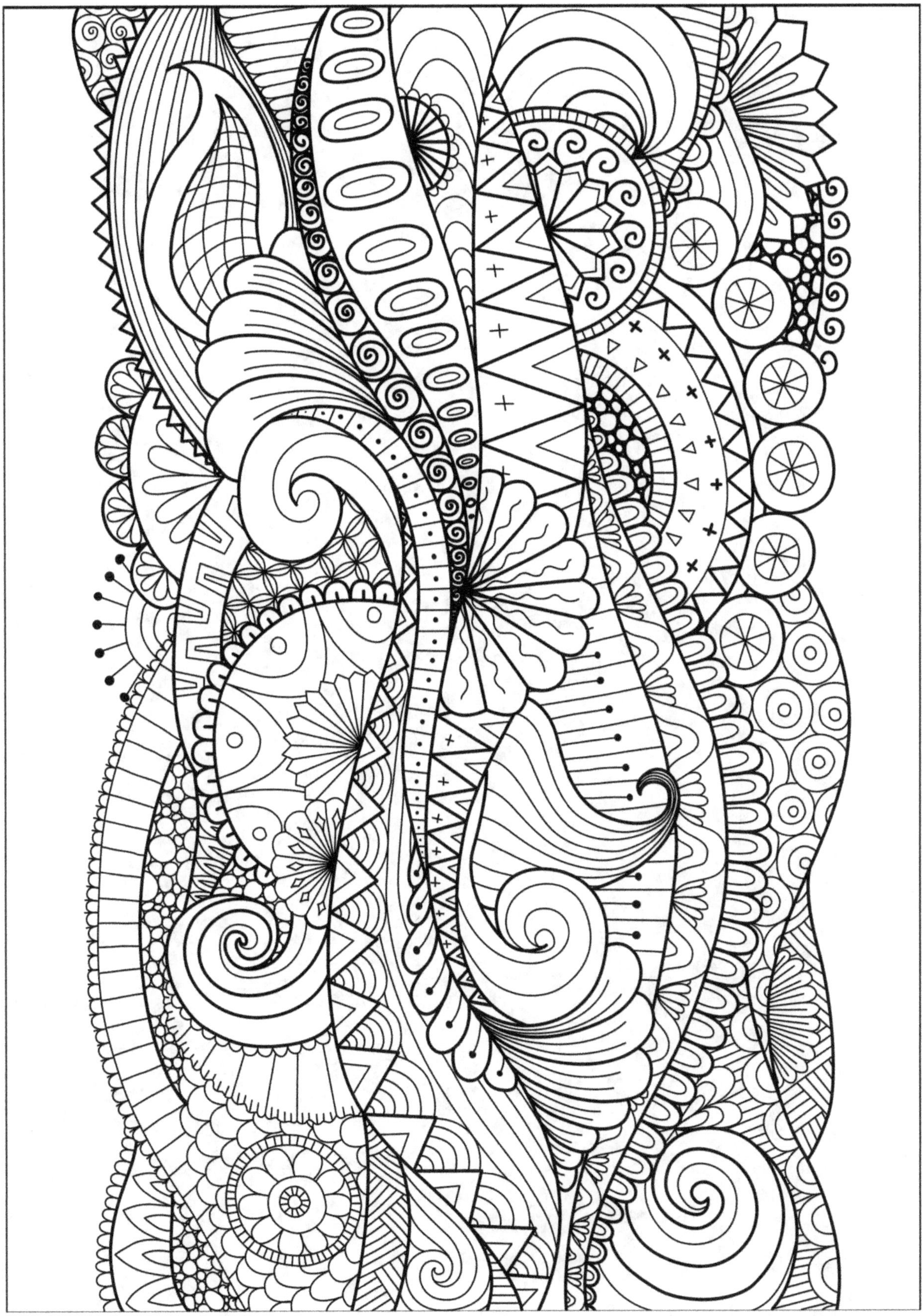

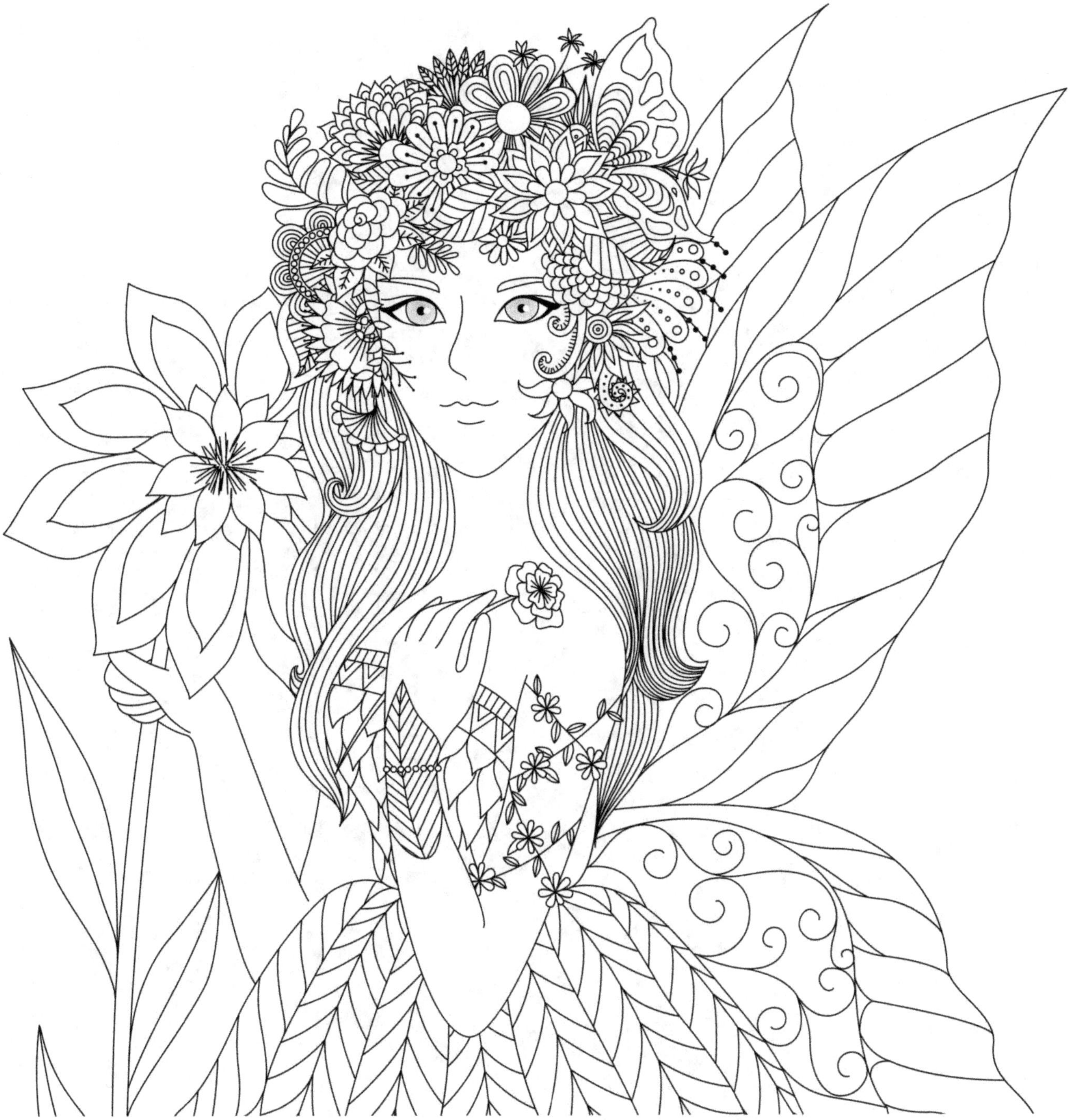

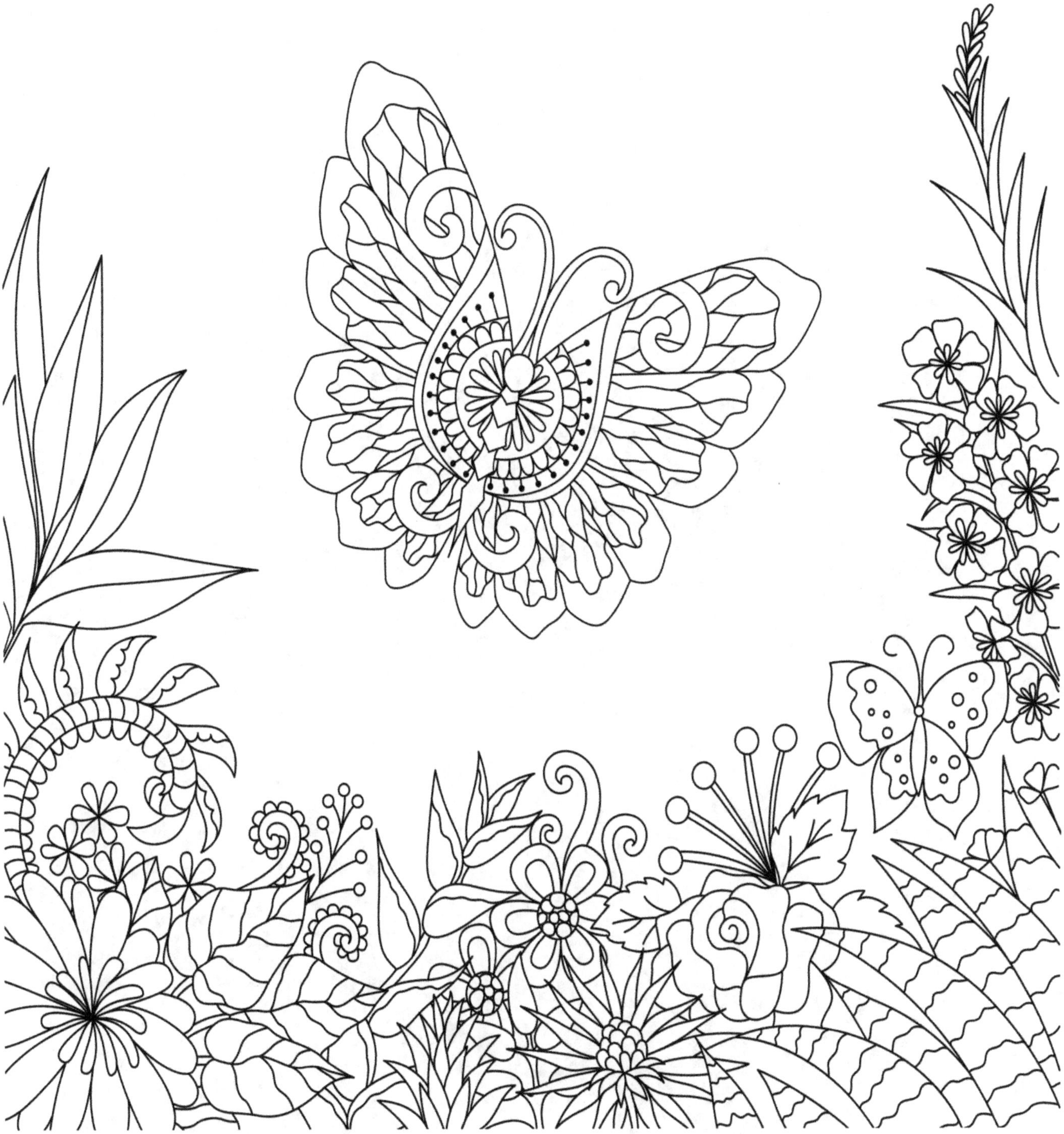

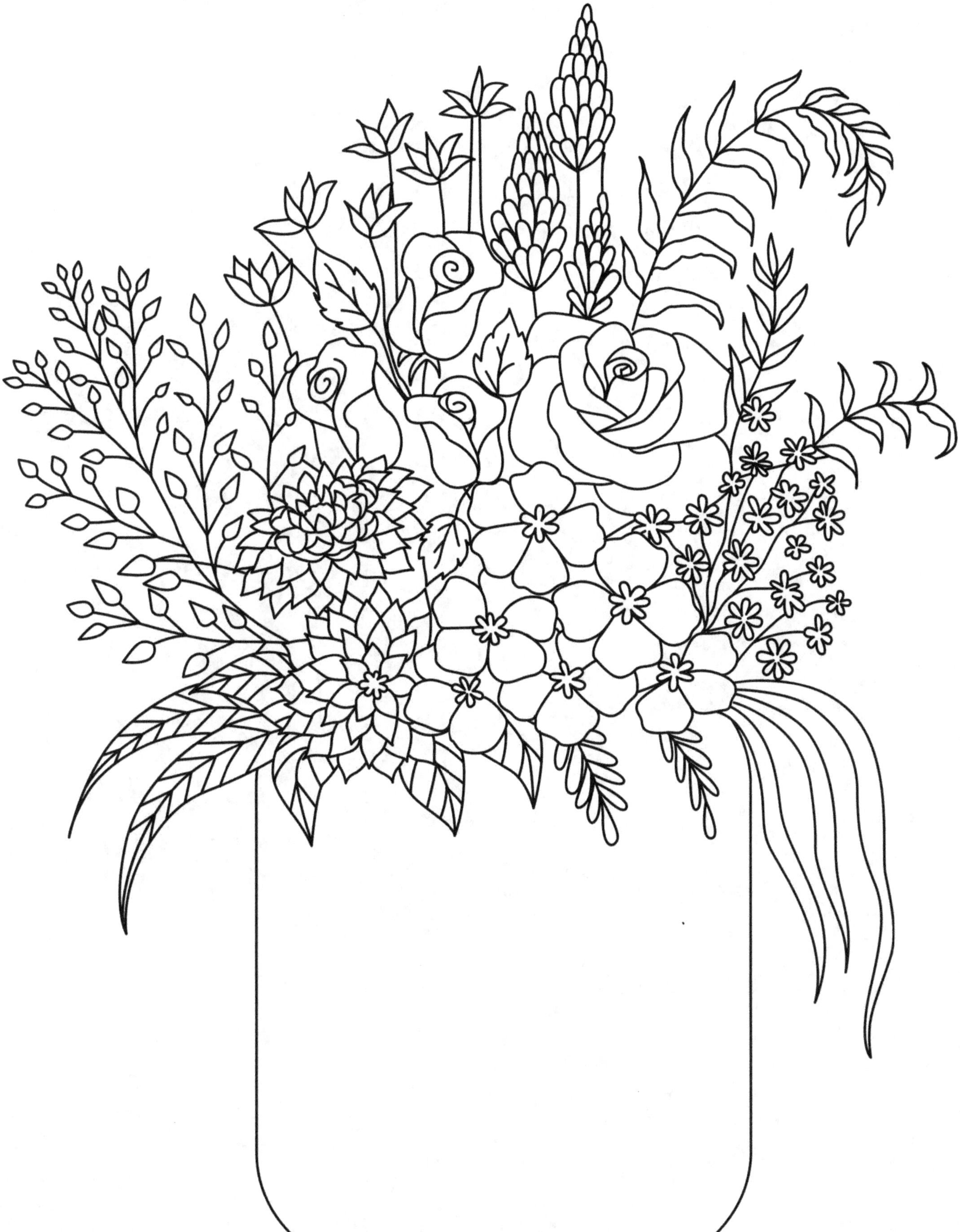

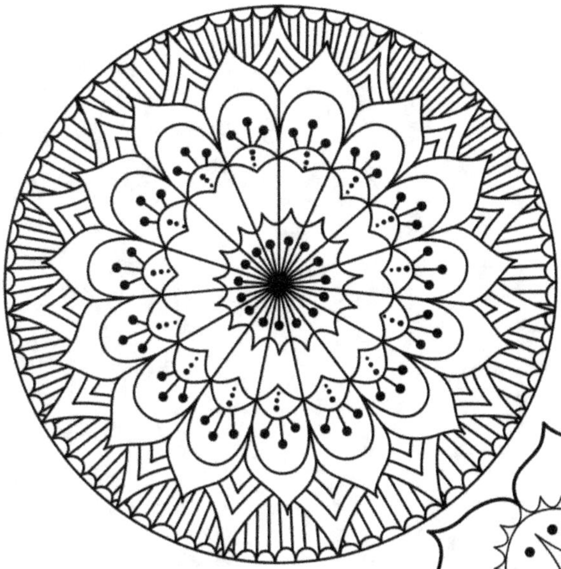
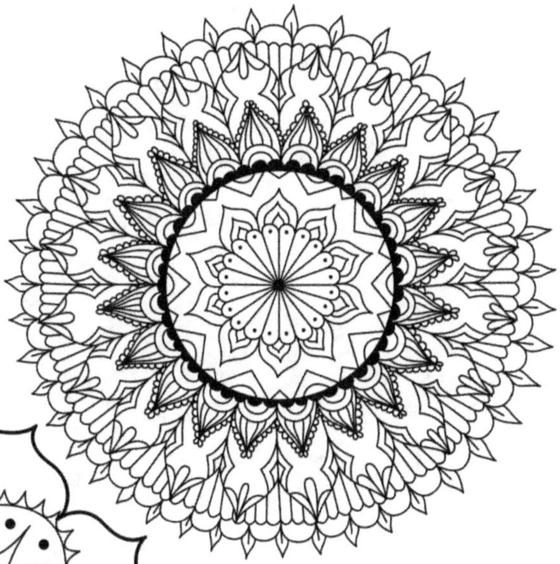
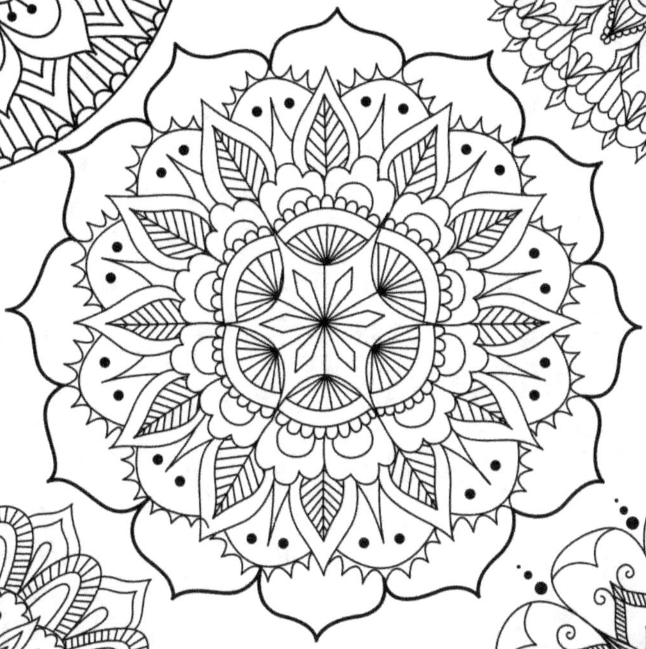
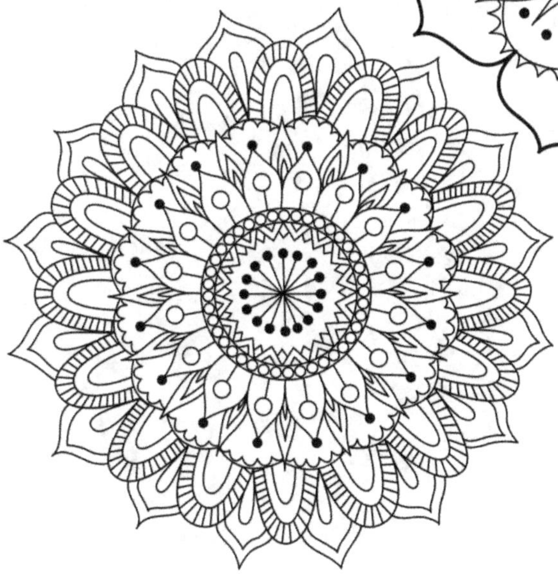
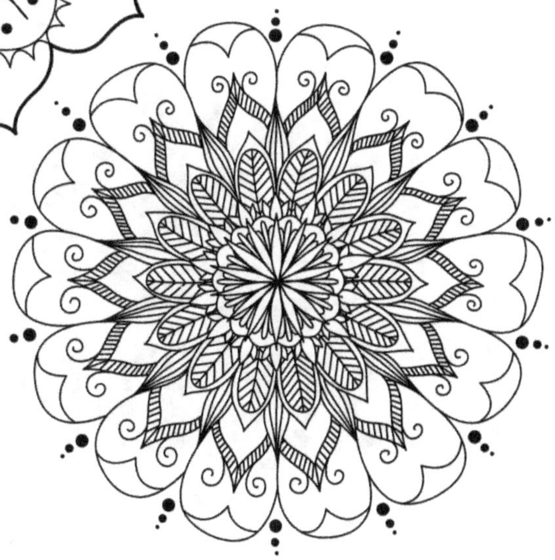

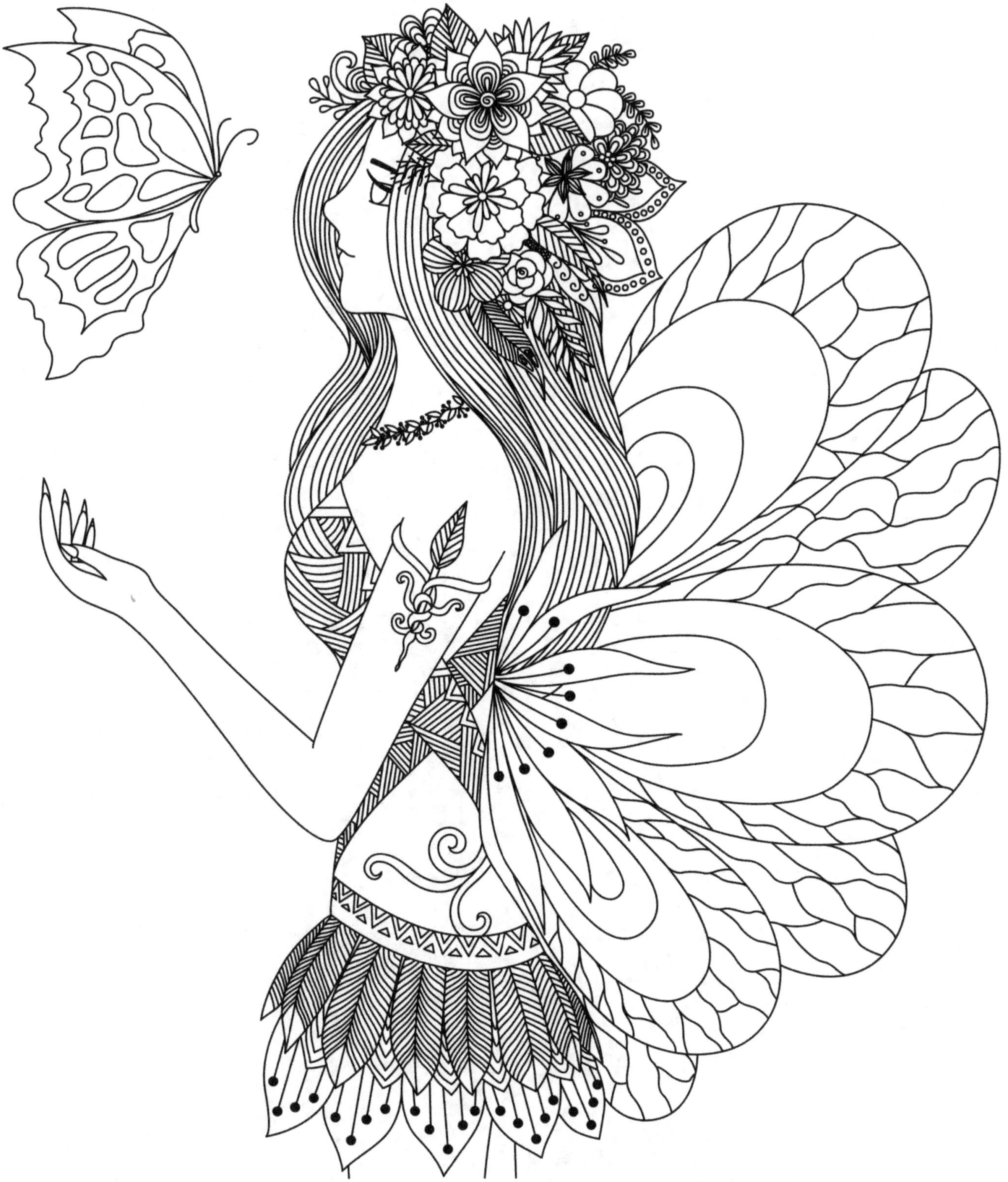

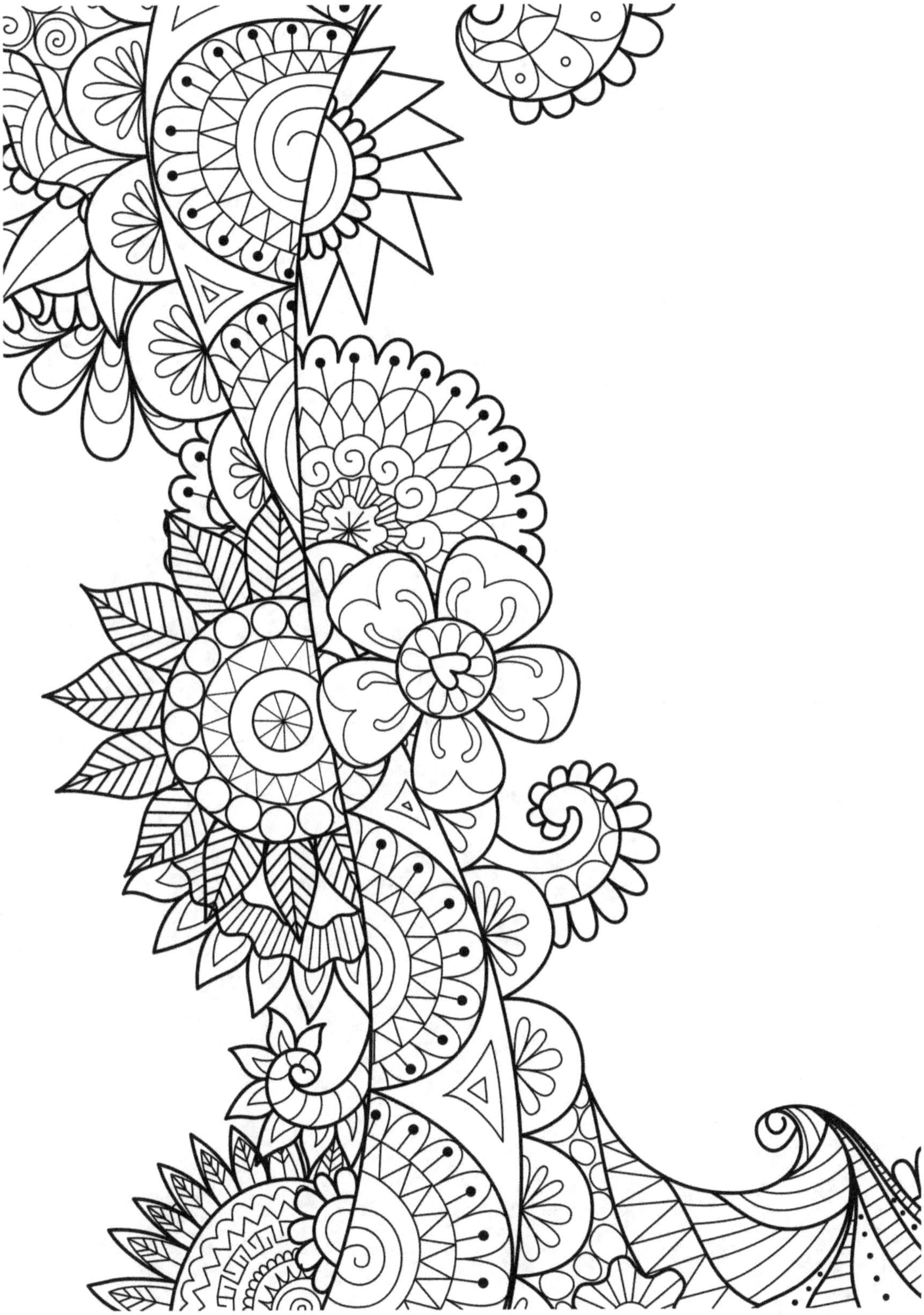

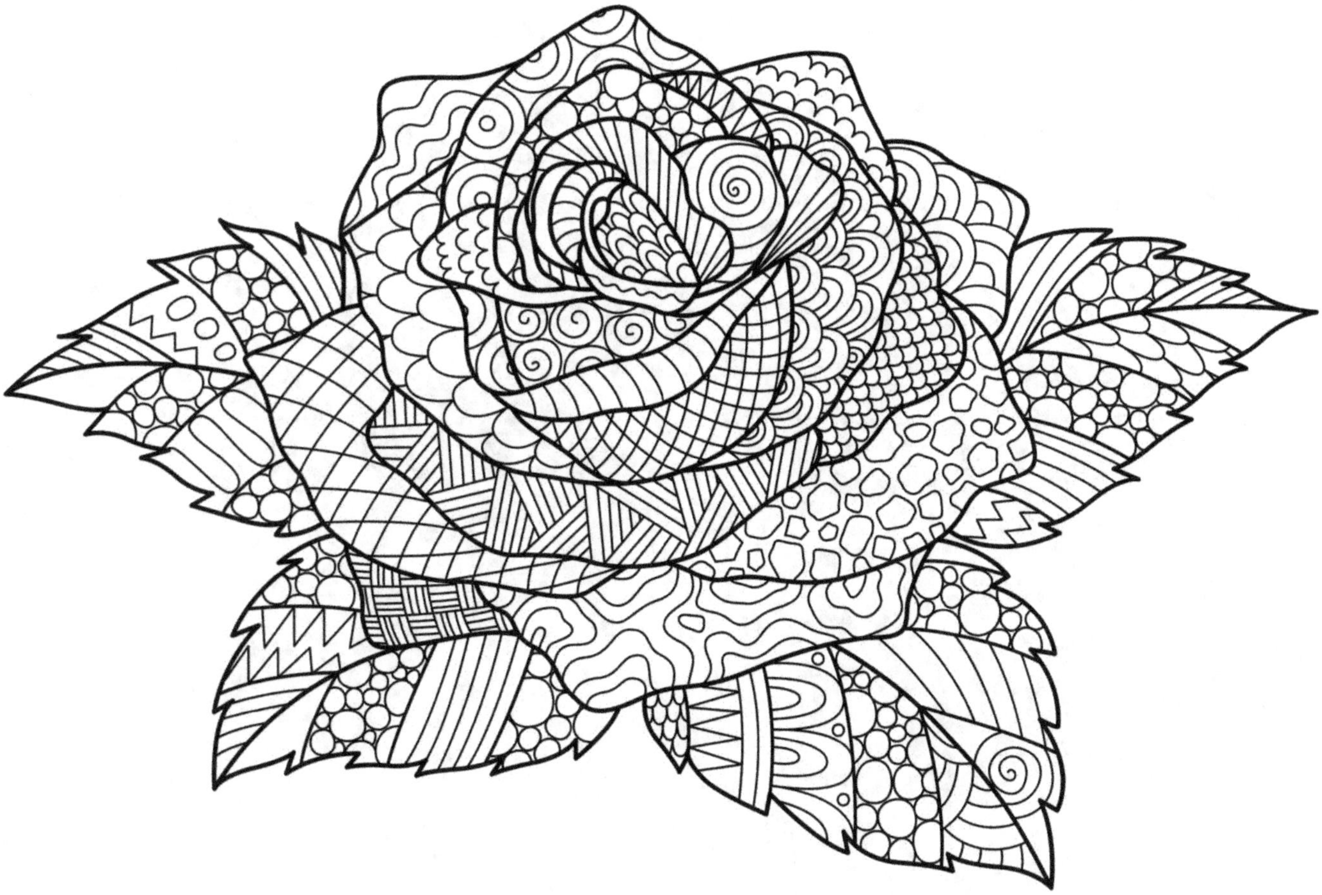

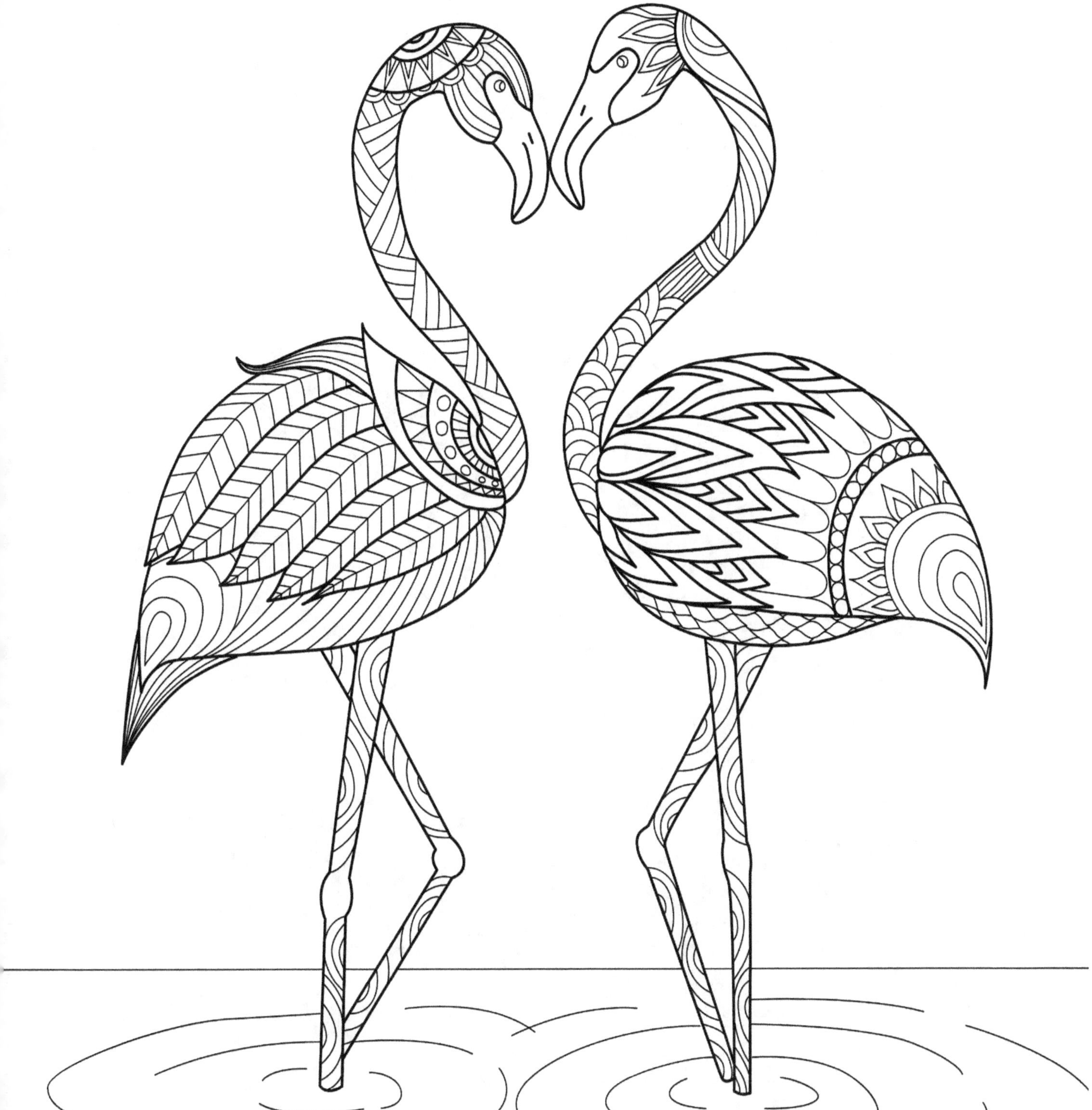

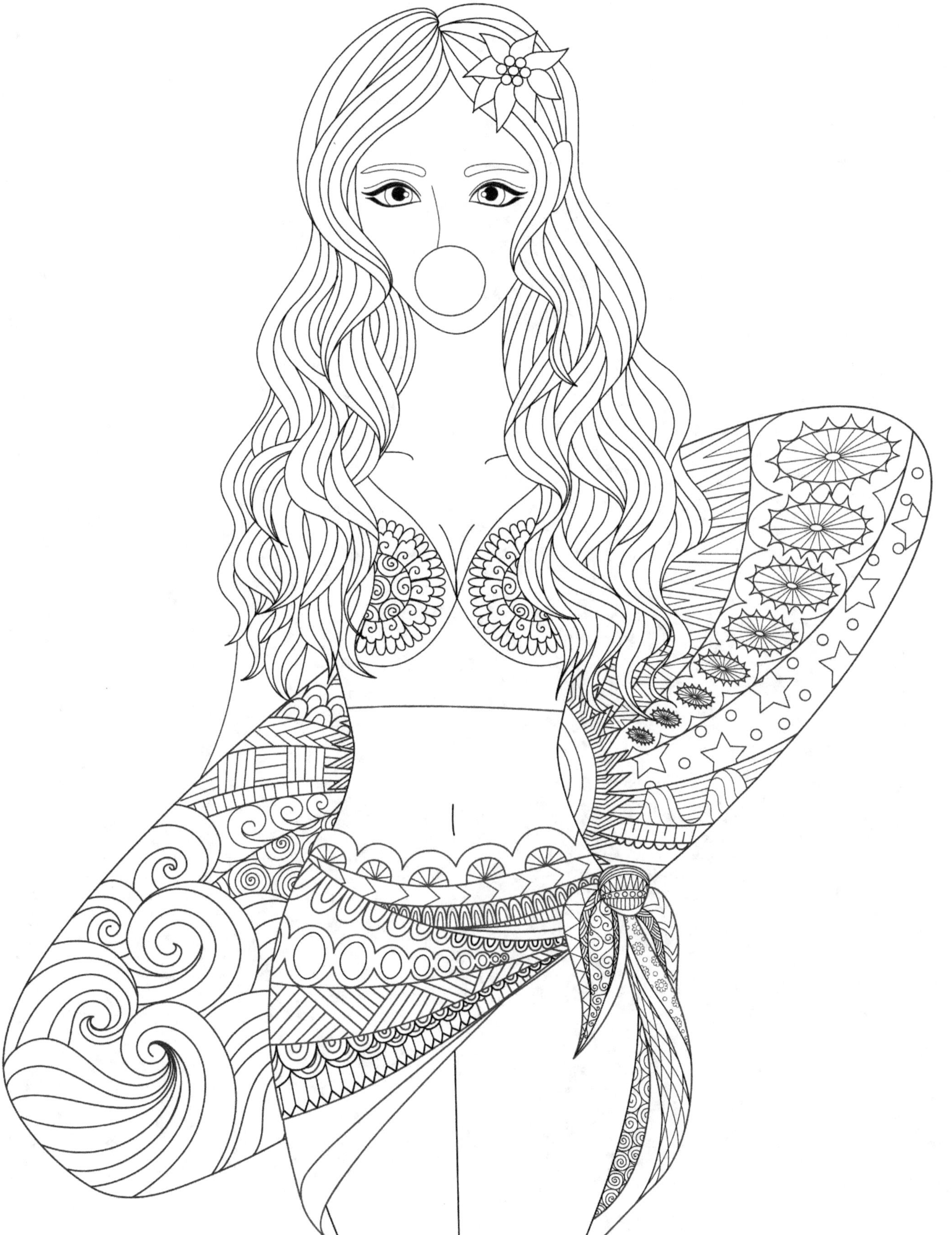

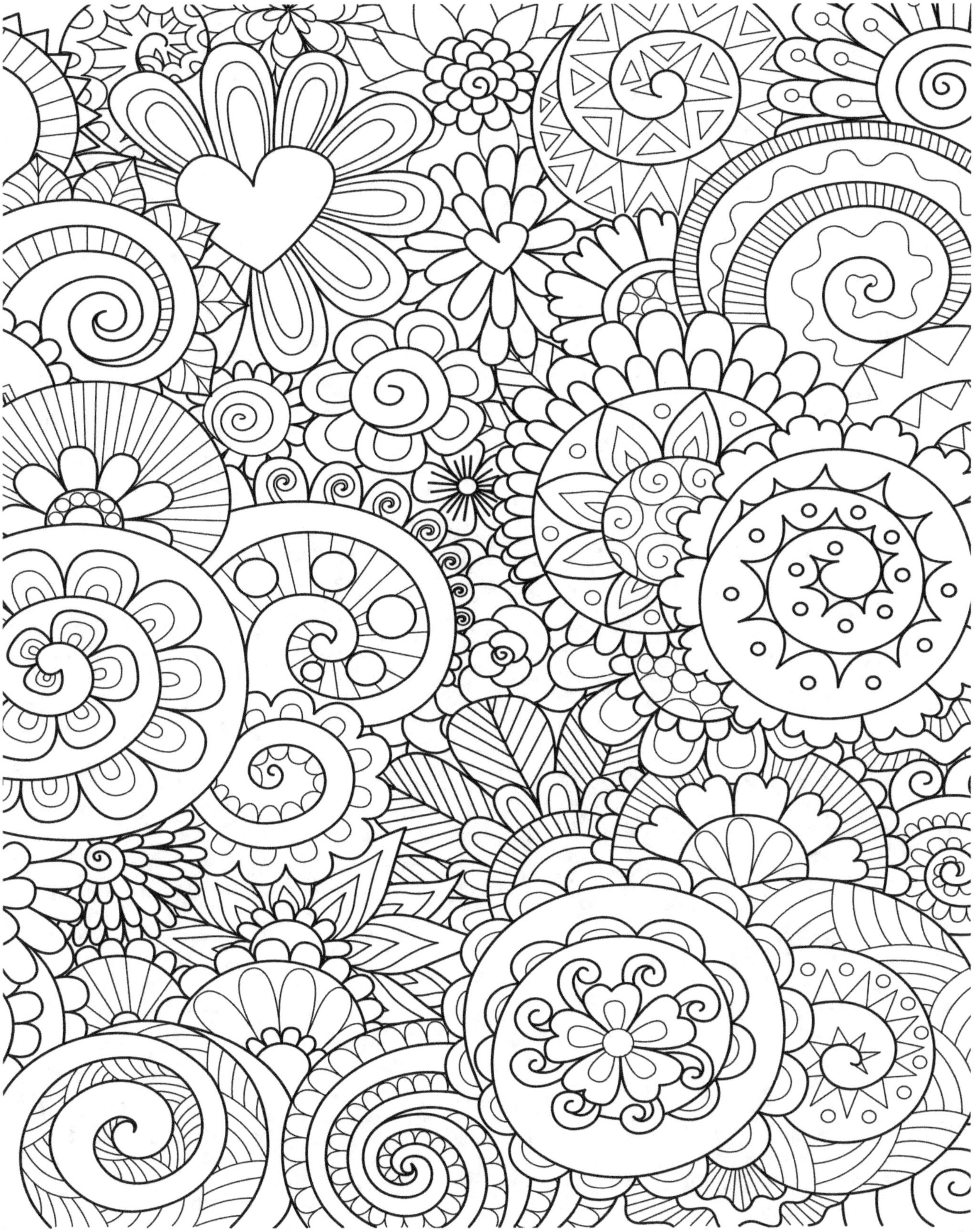

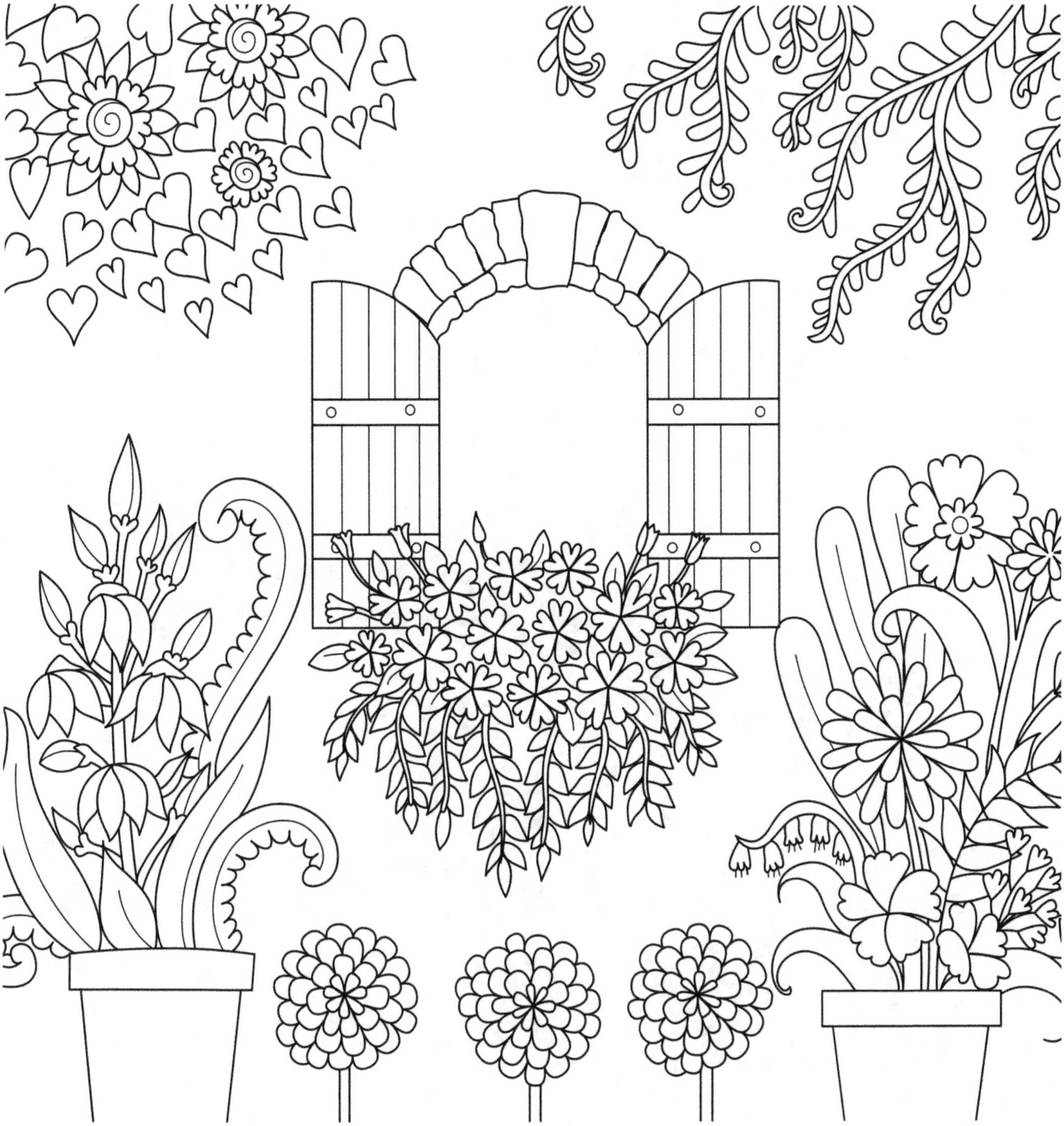

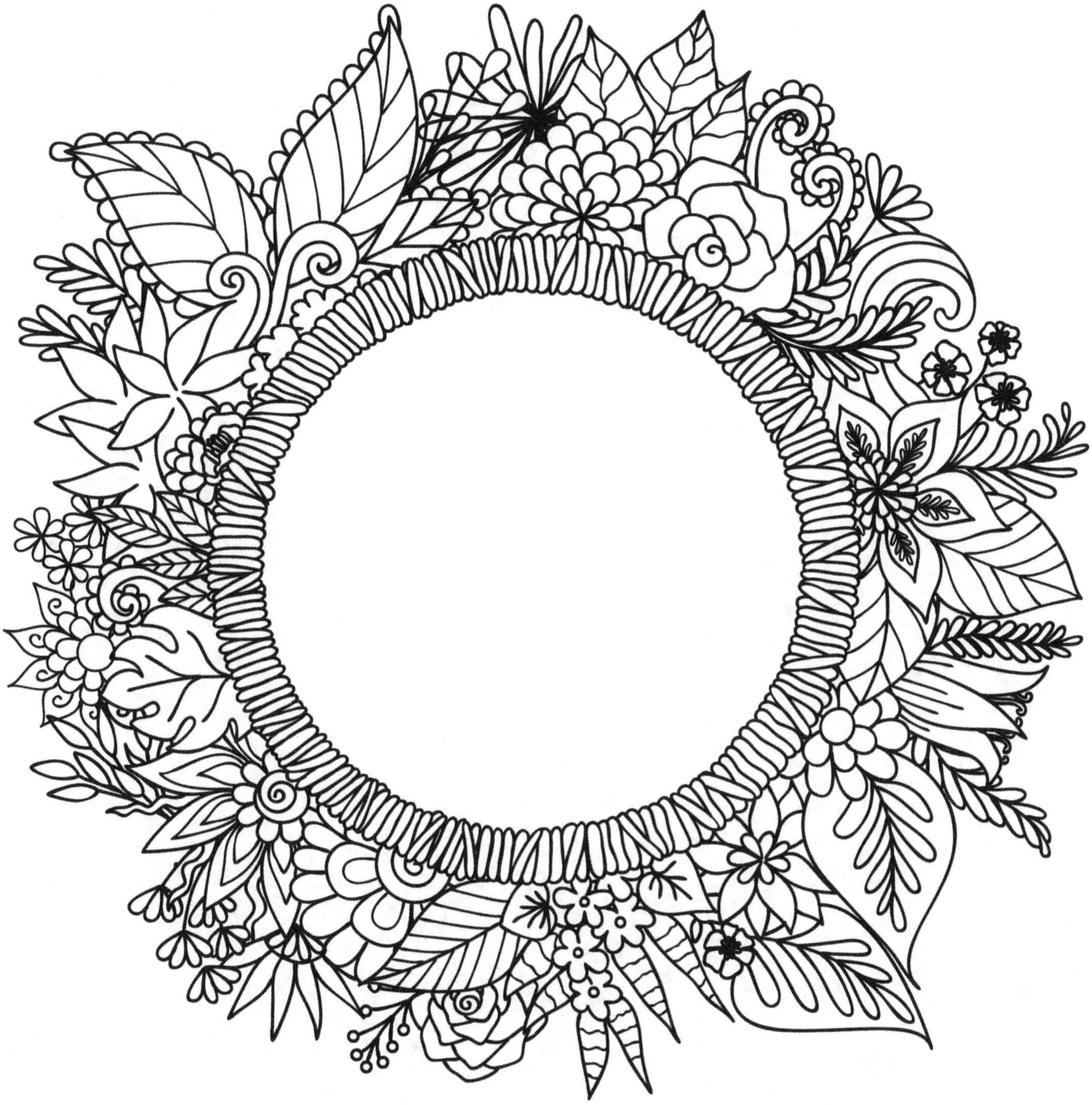

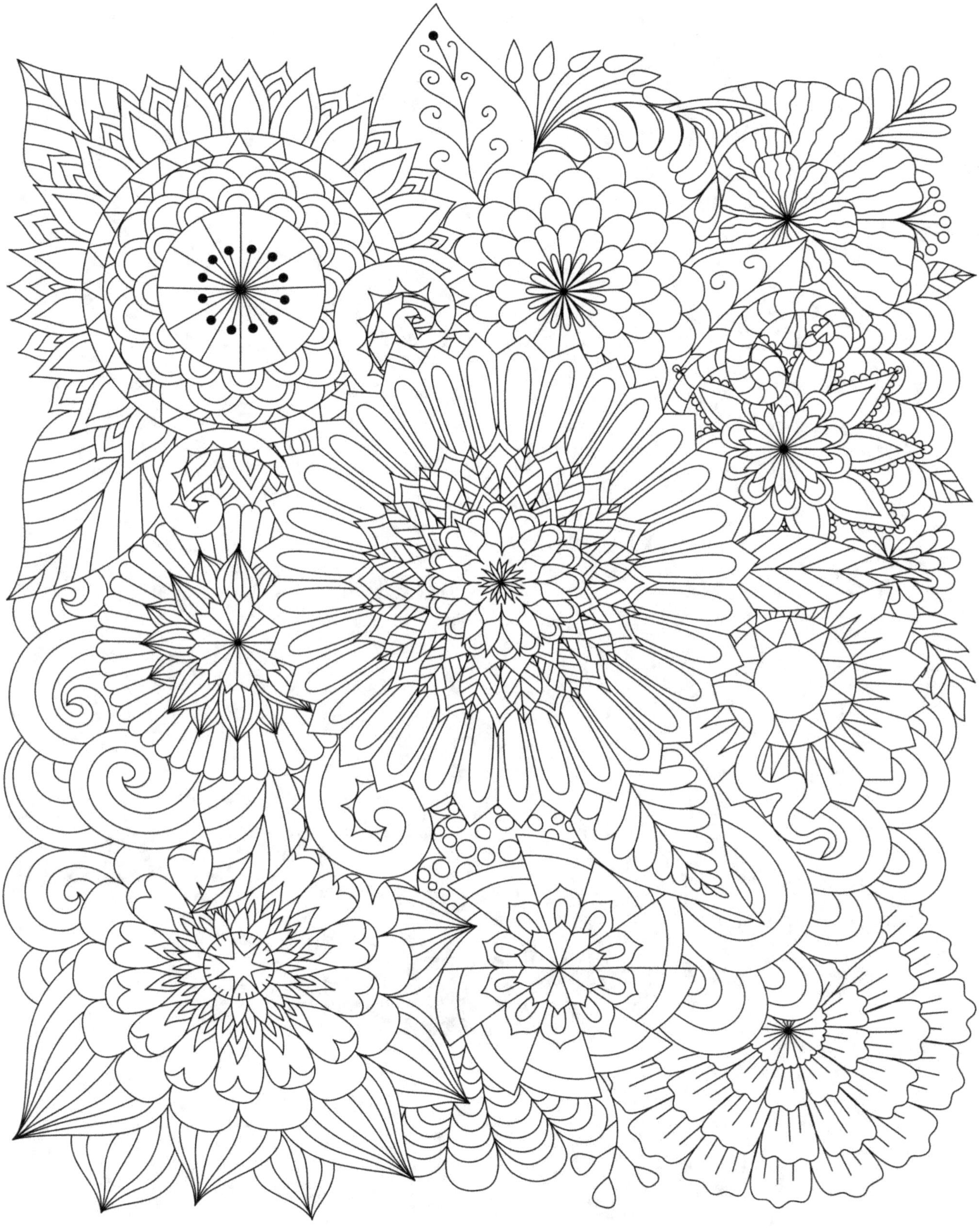

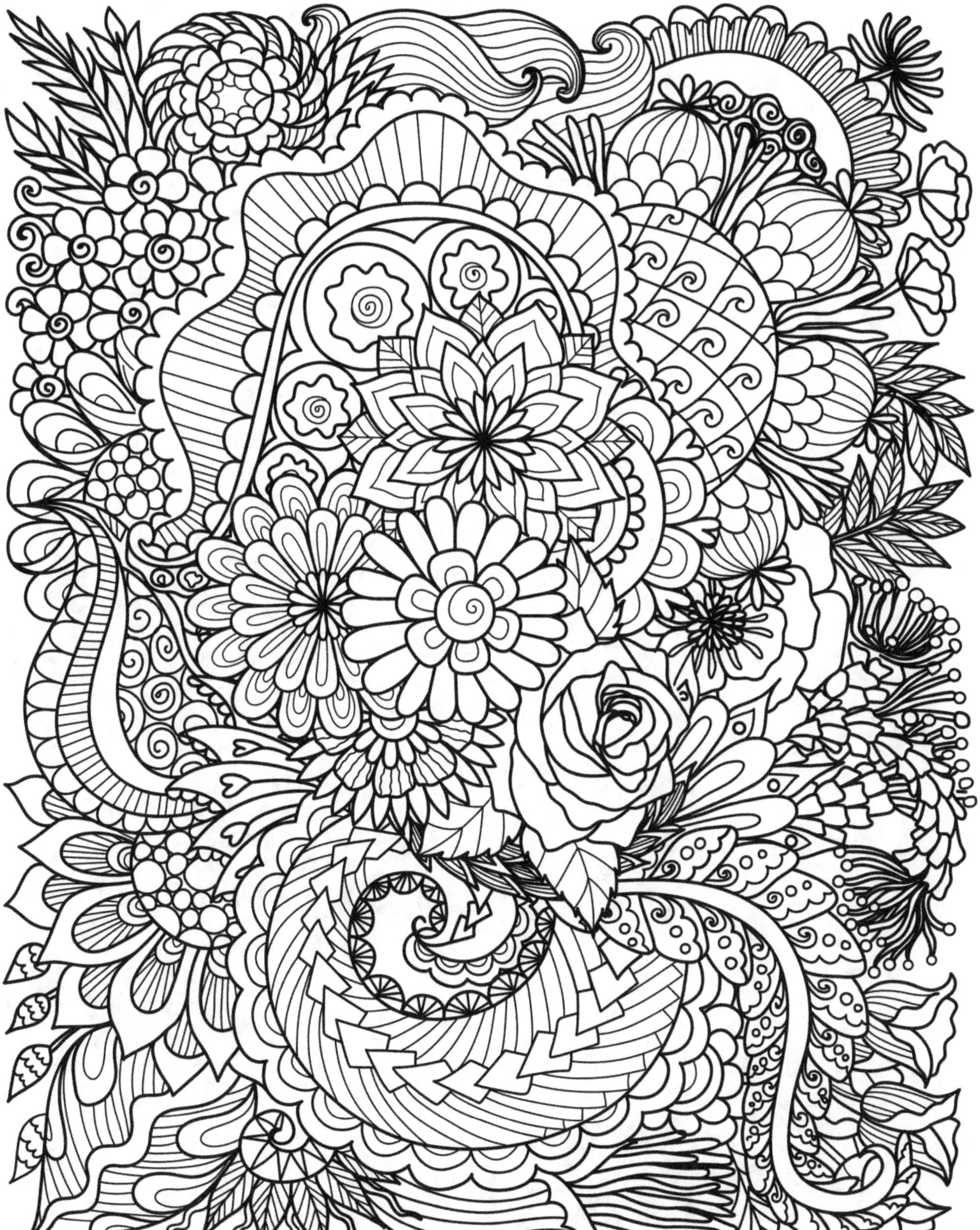

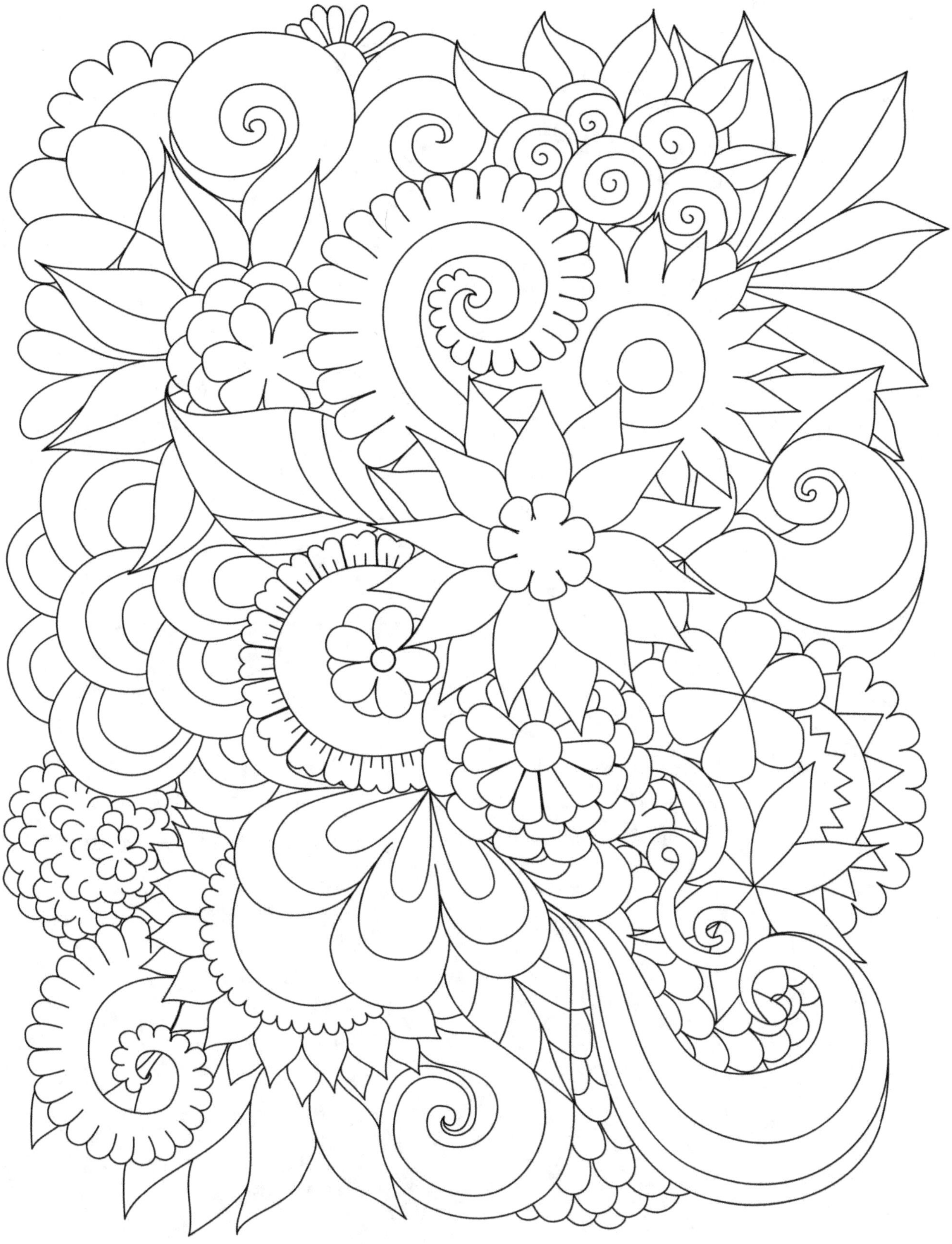

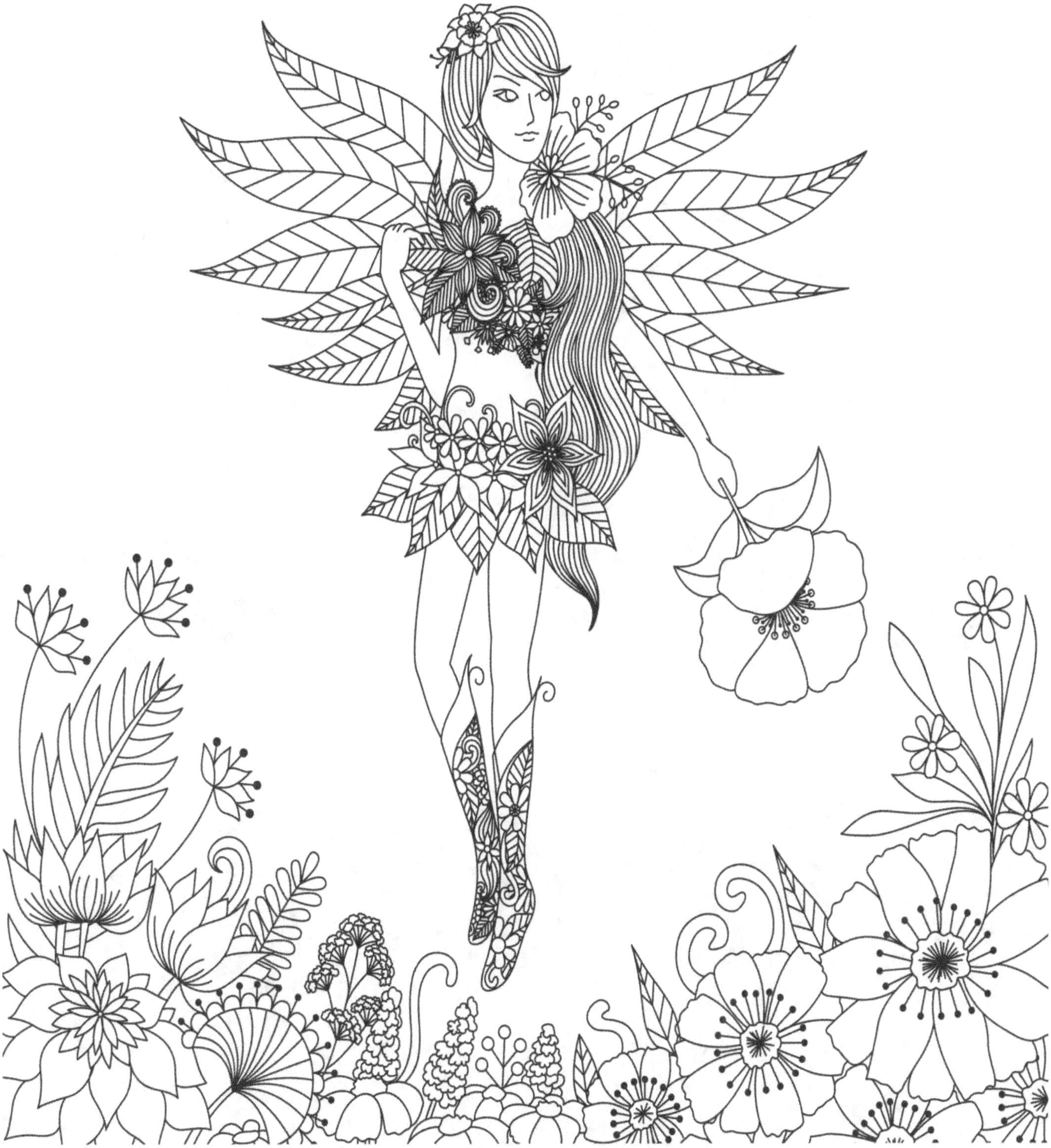

www.ingramcontent.com/pod-product-compliance
Lightning Source LLC
Chambersburg PA
CBHW081145170526
45158CB00009BA/2692
* 9 7 8 1 0 7 9 7 9 7 0 2 2 *